Bits and Pieces

Thoughts from a Life in Poetry and Prose

JOYCE HENEFIELD COLEMAN

BITS AND PIECES
THOUGHTS FROM A LIFE IN POETRY AND PROSE

iUniverse books may be ordered through booksellers or by contacting:

iUniverse
1663 Liberty Drive
Bloomington, IN 47403
www.iuniverse.com
844-349-9409

ISBN: 978-1-5320-6480-7 (sc)
ISBN: 978-1-5320-6479-1 (e)

Library of Congress Control Number: 2019901029

Print information available on the last page.

iUniverse rev. date: 01/30/2019

For Jacque and Jill

Also for my amazing grandchildren,
Kathleen, Zachary, Coleman, and Christopher

"Be the inspiration you are meant to be."

Preface

Everyone's life is a story—the story of a journey through joy and sadness, winning and losing, beauty and ugliness, good health and illness, love and hate. The challenge is to navigate through life and remain the person you were meant to be, to embrace life with all its joys and problems, and to make it a source of goodness, love, beauty, and happiness for yourself and for others.

Life and its cultures are constantly changing. Each generation faces its challenges and has its own cultural uniqueness. To older people the future may seem frightening, but to the younger generation it is exciting and challenging. Each generation must embrace its own beauty, love, and goodness, accept its own challenges, and navigate through losses—all the while becoming a positive force for change.

I have chosen to tell my story through poetry. I have loved poetry all my life. It speaks to my heart and soul. It is to be hoped that my children, my grandchildren, and those to come will glean insight into who I was and will be encouraged to tell their own stories and to be their own sources for change.

I truly believe that while we are on this earth we should do everything possible to bring joy, comfort, love, and positive change to others. We can do this in our own space and time. A smile, a hug, a fresh baked pie, a thank-you, or saying "good morning" or "have a great day" can lift someone's spirits and make a difference in their day. In doing these things, you will enhance your own life.

To Josh

The flowers have died, and we've said our goodbyes.
Your many friends each their respect did pay.
But there's pain inside and so many sighs.
When will the sadness go away?

We've begun again our lives to live
With an emptiness and loneliness inside
Because to you no more can we give
Our love or our joy, or our fears confide.

Although you felt no one would come
When for you the final bells did toll,
But come they did, and then some,
With sadness and grief deep in their souls.

Your final tribute you actually gave
Through feelings expressed and beauty shared
In the poems you wrote for your children brave
And for Maggie, for whom you deeply cared.

Although it may be trite to say
That you're gone but not forgotten,
Memories of you are with us each day
Because you were genuine and not store-"bought."

Written the month after Josh died in a tragic
accident on April 17, 1977

Masks

The protective wall and mask built so long ago and used to project contrived images of security and rightness is cracking,

Providing glimpses of a person I do not want to show, a person who has lost her affectedness.

Is there fear because this person I do not know?

My soul cries aloud for God's mercy and guidance, but I cannot feel his presence.

My very being begs for deliverance for I know that God is omniscient.

Am I being punished for past failures and indifference?

My inner being trembles with fear, confusion, and anxiousness to the point that I am not able to function effectively or see undistorted reality.

Constant depression mars hope for or expectation of happiness.

The struggle for emotional survival has drained me of essential vitality.

Why do I dwell in the pits of hopelessness?

Life has become joyless and meaningless, with piercing pangs of loneliness and desperateness, bringing fears that life has become rudderless

That life no longer has congruousness. Is my life meant to be purposeless?

At the crossroads of despair, as one ponders the choices to be made,

The heart and soul and mind are stretched to the limits one can bear in hopes of finding direction, truth, and hope instead of a charade.

Will my day of truth, hope, and direction ever come, or must I live in an illusion shifted by circumstance?

Written in late 1978 after an eighteen-month period wherein I lost five extended family members

Wild Paint

He is beautiful and free,
Allowed to breathe and to be,
Not shaped by human hands
Or kept enclosed in wire bands.

This high-spirited creation of God
Is made more lovely by the sod
That grows by leaps and bounds
Where earth and sky abound.

Hail to you! O untouched one,
Running and neighing in the sun.
Would that each of us could be
Unshaped by false conformity and free.

Written in the 1980s after watching a TV
program on the wild horses in the west

Juneau Glacier

Towering spheres of glistening white crystals.

Purity of genesis, a blinding purity not contaminated by humankind.

The air cleanses your very soul.

Absence of roads, tracks, footprints in the snow.

Feelings of continuity with earlier centuries.

Powerful sense of smallness.

An almost soundless environment broken by groans of ice moving, carving valleys and polishing boulders in its path.

Falling wedges of centuries-old ice reverberating; thunderous roars echoing through space.

Water falling gracefully and forcefully over and under thousands of feet of ice,

Following the course of least resistance.

Nature at work in its purist form, absent the forces of humankind.

Written after a helicopter ride to a glacier

View from the Top

Shimmering iridescent flakes of snow lie everywhere like a thick velvet cover.

Brightly clad skiers dot the landscape below, turning and bending as if dancing the minuet.

Snow-laden pine trees seem stoically bowed as if their burden were something to endure.

A lone wolf in the far distance cries aloud with a mournful quality that cannot be demurred.

All visible nature seems quietly at rest, contented and at peace with God and humankind,

Evoking a feeling of being blessed for this moment above the hustle and bustle of human beings.

With my skis in place and knees properly bent, the descending slope beckons me downward.

A gentle push brings feelings of exhilaration and amazement as I glide through time and space, onward and forward.

Skiing in Vail

Angel Child

You came into our life as a miracle,
Prayed for, hoped for, wanted desperately.
Bringing with you a quality somewhat lyrical
And a presence that said, *Touch me delicately.*

Your big dark eyes seemed to say,
I'll take you if you'll take me,
And from this very special day
A loving family we will be.

Years have passed since that first hour
When in my arms they placed your tiny form,
Radiating the beauty of God's finest flower
And making my heart exceedingly warm.

Each hour and each day thereafter
You have brought us such joy and happiness
By your love, your smiles, and your laughter.
Our hearts are full of gratefulness.

Each night when I lie down to sleep,
I thank God for the special blessing
Of giving you to us to keep
Until with him our souls are resting.

For Jacque

Sunday's Child

You were the child that was not going to be.
Three times I was told you would not be born alive.
But you were our special gift on a Sunday,
More than seven pounds in full overdrive.

Such joy and energy you brought into our home,
Quickly developing a precocious personality,
Exhibiting so many antics that I could write a tome,
Always evoking your own individuality.

With much love you were called "Jill the Pill."
You always had such a gentle and loving soul.
Watching you develop was an absolute thrill.
Throwing yourself into life was your goal.

You will always think outside the box,
But will meet whatever life brings head-on.
Difficulties will be looked upon as minor roadblocks;
"Can't do" is not part of your lexicon.

For Jill

The Girl with a Ball

The eyes are telling a story,
But what are they saying?
Is she afraid, angry, or feeling dilatory?
Perhaps she is fearful of disobeying.

What hopes and dreams will she desire?
What joys and sorrows are hers to face?
Will life feel like navigating a high wire?
Will she handle the hills and valleys with grace?

May life embrace her with experiences she cannot dream.
Help her to be unafraid to move ever forward.
Give her a sense of purposefulness and self-esteem.
Guide her across stormy seas, safely shoreward.

Thoughts about a picture of me at age three
holding a ball

Why, God, Why?

Their beautiful, innocent faces slide across the screen.
Six-year-olds in school, where they felt secure.
From this horrific act what are we to glean?
The crushing pain is so hard to endure.
Why, God, why?

Children waiting for Christmas, eleven days away.
A little boy says, "I just want Christmas to come. I don't want to die."
Each heroic teacher did her best their fears to allay.
They must also have been asking why.
Why, God, why?

How could another human being kill these precious souls?
What kind of an evil person perpetrates such madness?
In minutes, gone were their dreams, hopes, and goals.
We are all overcome with sadness.
Why, God, why?

Although separated from us now,
They will be loved and remembered forever.
Their families will sadly move forward.
This madman, their special bond he cannot sever.
Why, God, why?

Written after the massacre at Newtown,
Connecticut, December 2012

Tin Man

Down, down it came,
All 131 feet of tin and steel.
For eighty-four years it held the sky,
Casting shadows with the sun.

Time marched on and left Tin Man behind.
Rendered unsafe, incompatible,
Too expensive to maintain.
In 2013 Tin Man was no more.

Lingering now in hearts and on videotape,
You presided over Alamo Heights with dignity.
You were greatly loved and admired.
Hail to you, Tin Man!

Written when the iconic water tower named Tin Man was demolished on Monday, January 28, 2013. It had towered over Alamo Heights for eighty-four years.

My Mom

My mom is a wonderful person.
She takes me places and buys me things,
Although I may not like where she takes me or the things
she buys.
If she bought me three mounts, I wouldn't care, because it
is the thought that counts.
And I know is that she tries her best to bring me what I think
has zest. She's kind in heart, and that's a really great part.

My mom is a wonderful person.
She says sometimes that I don't appreciate all the things
she does.
I want her to know that is a bunch of buzz.
On occasion she gets mad, but we all know the cause of
that! (Me.)
Also she makes me feel so young,
Like a two-year-old just learning the English tongue.
But of course, she is like other mothers losing their precious
children to others.
This problem, though, I do understand.

When I become a mother, I'll probably have the same behavior at hand.
Despite all your different points of view,
I want to say this to you, Mother:

I love you.

> *Jacque is an amazing mom to two boys. She has mentioned that the boys do not always like what she buys and that she has to take it back. Life has a funny way of repeating itself.*

Peace

There are symbols representing you.
Gandhi wrote about and advocated for you.
Jesus identified himself as your prince.
Biblical scriptures invoke your name.
Why has humankind found you so difficult to sustain?

Do we not understand and respect our differences?
Do we not grasp hold of the beauty in those not like us?
Do we not see the commonality in all humankind?
Can we not accept other ways of worshipping God?
Will we learn to value and respect cultural differences?
Will we lose our own prejudices and stereotypes?

Biblically we are exhorted to live in peace with all people.
We are told that God is pleased when we live in peace.
May we find peace within ourselves.
May we "do" peace in our daily living.
May we bring peace and healing to our broken world.

I Still Remember

I still remember the old house,
The large front porch with rockers,
No electricity or plumbing,
Oil lamps providing light and shadows,
The water bucket on the back porch providing water.

I still remember the warm sand under my feet,
The feeling of sand between my toes,
Skipping down the hot sandy lane to the mailbox,
A world from long ago.

I still remember summer stays on the farm,
Picking peas, tomatoes, and fruit from the orchard,
Thumping watermelons trying to find a ripe one,
Watching our great-aunt wring a chicken's neck,
Which made eating fried chicken difficult.

I still remember canning days.
Everything was canned: fruit, vegetables, chicken, turkey.
There was a canning house in the backyard.

Shelling peas took a long time, as did shucking corn.
After a short time canning wasn't much fun.

I still remember the taste of cooked black-eyed peas,
tomatoes, and corn bread,
Smokehouse bacon and hot biscuits,
The red plum and wild grape jellies.
Boiled corn has never tasted as good.
And of course the pies cooked in the wood oven.

I still remember the magic of playing down by the creek,
Swinging on the grapevines and playing hide-and-go-seek.
We kept a watchful eye out for the Indians.
We were told that the last Comanche killed in the area was
just down the creek by the large tree.

I still remember that everyone in the whole family had a cow
named for them.
It was sad to know that Joyce would one day go to market.
A time or two we left a gate open and the cows got out.
Our great-uncle Ed was not pleased.

Uncle Ed came from the old country in December of 1876.
He was six years old at the time, speaking only German.
The voyage from Bremerhaven on the Frankfurt was long.
Indianola was their port of entry.
There they disavowed allegiance to Kaiser Wilhelm.
Texas was a new beginning with new opportunities.
They were in the United States of America, the New World.

> *As a third-generation American, I am so*
> *grateful to my great-grandfather for bringing*
> *his family to the United States. He was always*

proud to be an American, and he Anglicized the family name to be more American. He died before I was born. The farm was purchased in 1900 and stayed in the family until the mid-1990s. I sold the farm to pay for my mother's care during her twelve years of Alzheimer's disease.

Iron Man

A wry, mischievous smile.
A deep, abiding love for family.
Handsome through each stage of life.
A Depression baby with humble roots
Marked by the loss of his dad when twelve.

Never a braggart or pretentious.
Strong, solid, and determined,
Strong as the bond between the brothers three,
Jim, Jack, and Josh,
Each calling the other Iron Man.
Iron Man they were all their lives.

Ambitious as a human can be,
True to his word,
Careful in decision-making,
Helpful always to someone in need,

Determined to succeed in life,
Guided by an internal drive,

Halted only briefly by adversity,
Strengthened by challenge,

This man is greatly loved.
Smiling, teasing, generous, caring,
He wins the hearts of all who know him.
We are blessed by his presence in our lives.

For Jack

Boston Strong

Humanity at its best.
Human spirits rising,
Angels rushing to save lives.
Acts of compassion and kindness.
Horrific loss and body maiming.
Courage to face the unthinkable.

Boston stood strong.
The United States stands with them,
Giving millions in support and prayers.
A moment when everyone is committed.
"We will finish the race."
And finish the race they did.

Morocco

Desert hues on ancient walls.
Intricate woodcarvings carefully placed.
Brilliant tiles with remarkable designs.
Welcoming courtyards with blooming flowers.
A magical place of shadows and sand.

Narrow winding walkways begging to be explored.
Little shops with craftsmen selling their wares.
Spices, spices, and more spices
Releasing their fragrant smells,
Evoking thoughts of couscous and tagine.

Brightly covered watermen with cups all over
Bring a taste of water to thirsty people.
Singers dressed in gandouras,
Entertaining with song and dance.
Horsemen dressed for a fantasia,
Ready to show off their riding and shooting prowess.

A land of contrasts and ancient history
Steeped in tradition, religion, and cultural identity,
Proud of their place in time,
Struggling to embrace the twenty-first century,
Exotic, welcoming, and uncertain.
An unforgettable place to experience.

Where Is Sarah?

The wagon rolled westward,
Leaving Mississippi and headed for Texas.
There were rivers to cross,
Louisiana swamps to navigate,
Piney woods to meander.
South central Texas their goal.
Meager belongings in one wagon,
But opportunity lay ahead.
Three children began the journey;
Two arrived in Texas.
Baby Sarah died along the trail,
Buried beside the road,
Lost to time and history,
Mention of her found in an archive
A century after her death.

The question still remains:
Where is Sarah?
Most likely in the bosom of God.

Sarah was my great-aunt.

Horizon

The horizon comes ever closer.
Time marches forward.
So much still to be done,
Much to learn,
Dreams to fulfill.
A young me pondered purpose,
Longed for direction,
Looked for contiguousness in life,
Hoped to make a difference,
Sought to be my best,
Dreamed big dreams.
Aging brings a new perspective,
Reflection on life's blessings,
Feelings of loss for those departed,
Regret for the future I will not see,
An urgency to complete tasks,
Coming to terms with leaving this world.

Neptune

Hold your tall mast high.
You embraced the waters of Lake Travis.
Your classic beauty shone brightly.
You controlled the winds.

Three generations guided your sails.
You celebrated the Fourth of July,
Viewing fireworks overhead.
You navigated to dock parties,
Hosted birthday parties in the sun.
You rocked us to sleep.

Time marches on, but memories are forever.
You will always be in our hearts.
Sail on, sweet *Neptune*. Sail on.

Neptune *was Jim and Sybil's much-loved sailboat that we all enjoyed and loved. A new family now loves it.*

A Morning to Remember

It was five o'clock in the morning. I hurriedly dressed and quickly made my way to the forward bow of the ship. Mist was heavy, with glimpses of light beginning to make their daily appearance. Suddenly, I saw shadows of structures beginning to appear. For centuries these buildings have participated in this daily ritual. The ship slowly inched forward. As the light grew brighter and the buildings became more visible, my breath almost stopped. Such beauty and magnificence is rarely seen.

Venice was awaking to a new day. I tried as hard as I could to take in everything so that I could always remember this moment. The buildings, the misty morning sky, gondolas gently floating in their resting places, people beginning to stir, tower bells ringing in a new day. How magnificent this morning was for me. As I remember these moments again, my heart is racing and the images return. How marvelous it is to remember.

My Spiritual Framework

My spiritual framework and screen as a child were both calcified and rigid.

Hellfire and damnation were seared into my memory.

Fear of fire resulted in baptism twice.

I just wanted to make sure.

Years have passed since my Sunday school teacher had prayer for me because I was going to Trinity University, a Presbyterian university.

After I also attended Our Lady of the Lake College, a Catholic college, prayer was not offered again.

It was a politically volatile time between the Catholics and the Baptists in Texas.

John F. Kennedy, a Catholic, was running for president.

The whole world was going to hell.

I was puzzled because Presbyterians and Catholics had proven to be very nice and spiritual people.

They did not feel so different.

I felt that there were similarities; all believed in God, did good works in the community, and were my friends.

Uncle Glenn, of whom mother always said, "He is nice, but he is Catholic," became ever dearer to me.

These experiences began a lifelong journey of study as I tried to understand why we as human beings need to have or accept such rigid dogma.
The many wars and destruction of peoples and cultures over these rigid dogmas have resulted only in human pain. I cringe at the thought of all the suffering that has occurred because of calcified dogma.

I feel sad that even today rigid dogmas continue to rear their ugly heads, cluttering our airways, invading our politics, and attempting to force everyone to believe them.

Where are the lessons of history?

Haiku

Time is running out.
The horizon comes closer.
Departure will come.

Such joy this child brings.
I celebrate her success.
My blessings go forth.

What is life about?
Deeds done for someone in need,
Impacting someone's life.

Come, let us begin.
Become the change you desire.
Life is very short.

The time is now.
So much is uncertain.
Do not hesitate.

Songbirds are singing,
Squirrels are scurrying;
The morning awakes.

The sun is slowly rising;
A new day is beginning.
My heart is singing.

Her cute furry face
Brings smiles and love to my heart,
A wonderful joy.

Time marches onward,
The cycles of life complete.
Life is foreordained.

*Haiku are short poems that use sensory
language to capture a feeling or image.
They are often inspired by nature, a moment
of beauty, or an extraordinary experience.
Japanese poets often use haiku to express
something beautiful or poignant in the
environment. Traditional haiku consists of
three stanzas, the first with five syllables, the
second with seven syllables, and the third with
five syllables.*

A Grand Idea

A new country.
Everyone equal.
God-given rights.
Liberty from unreasonable control.

It was a grand idea,
Freedom to speak thoughts and ideas,
The right to pursue happiness,
Governance by consent of the people,
Laws based on accepted right and wrong.

It was a grand idea,
A shining light for the world,
No laws mandating religion,
No religious inquisitions,
The right to believe or not to believe.

It was a grand idea,
A place with opportunities,
A place to build a new life,

A place to fulfill dreams,
A land of milk and honey.

It was a grand idea,
But for all it was not to be.
Blacks and women were forbidden to vote.
Each black was counted as three-fifths of a person.
Children were not legally protected.
These rights would have to be won,
Fought for in a civil war,
Pushed for and demanded by advocates.
Bombings, arrests, beatings, fires, and dogs.
The grand idea was a dream not to be denied.

It was a grand idea.
Suffragettes made their demands.
Women rallied and raised their voices,
Wanting to be full citizens,
Wanting the right to vote,
Wanting their share of the grand experiment.

It was a grand idea.
The vote was granted.
Other rights and protections were yet to be won.
It would take another generation,
More marches and the raising of voices.

This grand idea so skillfully ordained
Shines ever brightly,
A beacon for the world.

Much won, more rights to come.
We must be vigilant.
What has been won can be lost.

It truly is a grand idea.

Cornhill

The winding road stretches over the rolling hills.
Family farms dot the landscape.
Fields lie ready for fall planting.
Church spires reaching toward the heavens,
Cemeteries providing eternal rest.
Sounds of polka music waft across the valley,
Accordions, guitars, and drums playing polkas,
Celebrating the music of the old country.
Children playing games, waiting for lunch.
Old people chatting about the past,
Expressing love of the land and family,
Waiting for barbecue, sausage, and trimmings,
Keeping an eye on the kolaches and apple strudel.
It is festival time again in Cornhill.

The Oak

Gracefully toward the heavens your limbs wind,
Welcoming the morning light,
Admiring the setting sun.
Leaves that rustle softly
Or blow with the wind.
Roots firmly established in limestone and dirt,
Awaiting rain and nutrients and the Texas sun.
You greet me each morning
At the beginning of my day.
You make me smile
While sipping tea and viewing your majesty.
Oh the stories you could tell.
Native Americans, settlers, Texicans, cattle, and goats.
Each in time passed along your path,

Perhaps sat in your shade,
Admired your beauty, as do I,
Dreamed of what this land could be.

> *This lovely oak stands outside my kitchen*
> *window.*

Our Journey

Oh what a journey.
Together we've traveled
Up the high roads,
Through the valleys,
Always striving, dreaming, growing,
Together building a future,
Making things better,
Following dreams.
Life is not always kind.
Boulders and closed doors,
Loss and challenges,
Strengthening our determination,
Testing our mettle,
Shaping our vision.
Now in the twilight years,

We reminisce about the past,
Feel blessed, and give thanks
For all who shared our journey.
Our final journey awaits.

Loss

You are always lurking,
Waiting to strike.
For some you are overwhelming.
Others stoically accept your deeds.

Your actions are puzzling.
Some are struck down so young,
While other, old souls linger
Beyond their mind and body's desire.

Mass losses are incomprehensible.
So much pain inflicted.
Humankind struggles to understand
Any mind that courts you.

Thinking Out Loud

They are thoughts that spring from my soul.
They reinforce lists, ideas, and things to do.
My daughter says, "Mom, are you all right?
Are you aware that you are talking to yourself?"
I am not talking to myself.
I am reinforcing my thoughts.
I am writing poetry in my head.
I am editing in my head.
I am simply thinking out loud.
This explanation is much better
Than admitting I am getting old.

Evilness

It is sobering to ponder the evil in this world.
My heart aches with sadness at the images unfurled.
In video, digital, and sound they shake my soul,
The horrific acts their power to extol.
What can possibly justify such slaughter and rape?
Confining thousands with no means of escape,
Left to die of heat, hunger, and thirst,
Looked upon as people cursed.
My mind cannot understand such evilness.
The Yezidis were simply living on their ancient land.

It's the Little Things

Stop, listen, and look around you.
The birds are chirping,
Nature's gift of a morning symphony,
So many sounds perfectly blended.
Close your eyes; breathe deeply.
It's the little things that matter.

Stop, listen, and look around you.
Nature's colors are stunningly beautiful,
A beautiful blue sky above,
Shades of white and gray in the horizon,
Many shades of green all around.
It's the little things that matter.

Stop, listen, and look around you.
Feel the gentle breeze.

See the swaying of the trees.
Hear the chirping of the birds.
Say, "I am glad to be alive."
It's the little things that matter.

Majestic Oaks

I gaze upon your twisted limbs
Winding their way upward,
Reaching toward the heavens.
Galaxies of stars shine back at you.
For centuries you have kept watch.
How many shooting stars have you seen?
Do you ponder the vastness of the universe?
Do you wonder about the purpose of it all?
How many storms have you weathered?
I see so many twists and turns in your limbs,
Cuts from loss of branches.
Still you stand with roots deeply grounded,
Providing shade and comfort,
Sharing your beauty and majesty,
An inspiration for those who stop and wonder.
Humankind has much to learn from you.
We are each bruised, broken and scarred.
So many storms to weather in life,
Twists and turns to be taken,
Losses to survive, lessons to learn.

But like the oak, we can survive.
We can heal from the storms of life.
We can look ever upward.
We can grow our roots deeper.
We can serve as an example to others.
And in the end, we will have served our purpose.

furry Babies

Thank you, God, for furry babies,
Little brown eyes full of love,
Glances of reassurance.
My soul smiles deep inside.
Their unconditional love wraps around my heart,
Forcing a smile from my sad face.
They instinctively know I need them.
The weight of sadness somehow lifts.
Their playful love provides reassurance and comfort.
All is not lost.
Love abounds.
We need each other.

For Lolita and Yogi

Rio Medina

At dusk I wander along the Medina River.
Shadows of the bald cypress cast their spell,
Changing with the setting sun.
I sometimes feel the presence of spirits,
Perhaps ancient Native Americans who found respite here
Ate pecans, wild onions, and grapes,
Feasted on deer and wild turkey.
Perhaps it is a Spaniard, or
Maybe a Mexican, a French explorer, a German settler, or
a Texican

All left an imprint on this land.
All can say, "I was here."
We celebrate their bravery and sacrifice.
We celebrate the legacy we have been given.
Oh beautiful river and land of mine,
Tell me the story.
Tell me about Garza's crossing.
Tell me about the Battle of the Medina fought downstream.

Tell me about Santa Anna crossing nearby to do his dreadful
deed.
Tell me about the Herrera-Ruiz family.
They once owned this land.
Some are buried nearby.
One signed the Texas Declaration of Independence,
One the first Alcalde of San Antonio
Made to identify and bury the Alamo dead.
A family who helped change the course of history
Oh land and river, I ponder my role.
What have I added to your story?
Have I made you better?

*Dedicated to the Herrera-Ruiz family. Some
descendants still live nearby.*

*This poem was selected for artistic
rendering as part of the San Antonio, Texas
Tricentennial celebration.*

Place des Vosges

A manicured oasis.
Grandeur around simplicity.
Perfume in the air.
Children running, skipping, playing.
Old people sitting hand in hand,
Remembering, reminiscing, and dozing.
Lovers sprawled on blankets,
Lost in each other.
Dogs looking for their territory.
Tourists pointing cameras.
Daily life all around.
King Louis XIII rides high upon his steed,
Eternally overseeing this realm.
Fountains spray cooling water,
Creating a restful sound.

Carefully formed tree arbors
Bring respite from the Parisian sun.
Victor Hugo drew inspiration here.

A favorite park in Le Marais, Paris

Life

Life happens.
The months and years
Come and go.
One day you ask,
"Where did the time go?
How did I get this old?"
It all seems unreal.
You ponder your life's events.
So many happy times,
Sadness for all the losses,
Regrets for the opportunities not taken,
Gratefulness for those who inspired you,
Pride in your family,
Struggling to accept being alone,
Grateful for a long life,
Waiting for the final curtain.
Quite a ride it has been.

Morning

How I love the morning.
It is a new beginning,
Bringing opportunities to just *be*,
To soak up the morning light,
To reminisce about the past,
To remember those who blessed your life,
To plan for a new day.
Two precious Yorkies light up my spirit,
Four brown eyes sharing their love.
When our hearts are anxious or sad,
Morning can bring a new perspective,
Strengthen our resolve,
Open our eyes to new possibilities,
Grant us peace within ourselves.
This morning as I gaze across the horizon,
I see that the lake is sparkling and beckoning,
The hills are glowing in the morning light,

The sun is casting shadows, and
The trees are momentarily still.
I breathe in the morning deeply.
How good it is to welcome a new day.

Now That You Are Gone

Now that you are gone,

I feel your presence around me.

My heart longs for one more hug,

A kiss good night, your silly grin.

For almost fifty-nine years we worked side by side,

Not always agreeing, but always loving each other.

You accomplished so much in your lifetime.

You made me the woman that I am,

Sometimes kicking, mad, hurt, crying.

You always said, "You can do it."

As I look around me, I see your handiwork.

I feel your presence.

The gardens you and Jacque designed,

The large heart sculpture in the arbor:

Hidden Valley.

Our amazing family.

All remind me of your big and loving heart.

The day will come when we will be together again.

That journey we began so long ago

Will one day be complete

And we will hold hands again, this time forever

Until then, I will hold you in my heart.

A Tribute

We held hands and walked along the Seine,

Crossed the lock bridge and watched the lights shine from the Eiffel Tower.

We walked the ancient streets of Rome,

Threw coins in the Trevi Fountain

Imagined the ancient Romans living their lives,

Marveled at the works of Michelangelo, Botticelli, et al.

We trekked the streets of Athens, Mykonos, and Delos,

Walked the ancient wall of Dubrovnik,

Rode a gondola through the canals of Venice,

Stood atop Tel Megiddo overlooking the valley of Armageddon,

Imagined the ancient battles and the prophesized one to come.

We floated in the Dead Sea,

Stood atop Mount Masada as an Israeli jet tipped its wing in respect for the past.

We walked the ancient streets of Old Jerusalem,

Remembering the Bible stories we learned as children.

We walked along the Sea of Galilee,

Remembering Jesus's walk and Peter fishing there.

Magical Florence with its history and art touched our hearts.

Standing alongside Michelangelo's *David* was unforgettable.

One could almost see the muscles flex.

Such perfection from a reportedly lesser grade slab of marble.

We cruised the Baltic, the North Sea, the Kiel Canal, and the Rhine River.

We visited towns and villages along the way.

We marveled at the art in the Hermitage,

Toured the Palaces of the Czars, and marveled at the beauty of Saint Petersburg.

We were in London when Princess Diana died.

The collective sadness of the day was unforgettable.

You relished your Irish heritage in Dublin,

Touring with your buddy Mike Kelly,

Learning about the Coleman clan.

Perhaps you and Mike are reminiscing in heaven.

Your last trip was through the Panama Canal,

Something you always wanted to see.

How blessed we have been to see the world we live in.

I am eternally grateful for the opportunity to see the world with you

I am also grateful for the lessons I learned from you:

The value of hard work,

The need to save for the future,

How priceless family is,

How not to give up when difficult times occur.

You were the strength that got me through difficult times.

You were there during my medical emergencies.

You got the whole family through the tragic death of Josh.

You stepped forward and did what needed to be done.

You were a loving son to your mother and helped the whole family cope with her illness and death.

You were my strength during my mom and dad's deaths.

You made many sacrifices without one complaint.

You taught me never to give up and just find another way.

We stood looking at the loss and devastation of the 2002 flood.

All I could do was cry.

You said, "Let's get to work."

And so we did.

We rebuilt little by little with Mark and Teri's help.

Perhaps your most important gift has been the gift of family.

You have treasured and loved Jacque and Jill all their lives.

You have loved Rosalee, Daliya, Mia, and Bella and included them in the family.

Your grandchildren Kathleen, Zachary, Coleman, and Christopher are your treasures.

You were amazed by and proud of all their accomplishments.

You told a nurse, "Grandson graduates A&M."

You were filled with Aggie pride even though you professed to be a Longhorn.

You have been an inspiration to your many nieces and nephews, who love you very much.

You have so many friends, some of whom have known you since high school, who love you, admire you, and celebrate the person you are.

You were an inspiration to all who knew you. We grieve for your loss but celebrate your life.

You always said you were just a country boy at heart. Well, dearest Jack, you were one very special country boy.

Au revoir. You are loved.

Rain

The rain is gently falling,

Soaking the parched earth.

The summer heat has been brutal.

Natural plants have struggled to live.

We have asked God for relief.

Today he granted our wish.

Pundits pontificate about climate change

Elected officials do nothing.

Natural landscaping is now the norm.

I truly wish to be a good steward.

This planet called Earth is amazing,

But humankind is ravaging its beauty.

Today I breathe in the washed air.

Thank God for this respite from the heat.

I recommit to caring for my piece of earth.

Come and sit awhile.

Come and Sit Awhile

Breathe deeply.

Take in the beauty all around.

Find beauty in the small things, the old things.

Feel your heartbeat.

Relish this place and this moment in time.

Listen for the sounds all around,

So much hustle and bustle.

Set it aside for the moment.

Close your eyes.

Feel your heartbeat.

Remember, you are special.

You can make a difference.

Good Night

Here I stand on the precipice of time.

The western sky is awash in magnificent color.

The hills are covered in evening light.

Where has the time gone?

This gift of earth follows an ordained path,

Spreads its beauty everywhere.

The hills around me absorb the light,

Casting shadows here and there.

Ever so slowly the glorious light slips over the horizon.

The magnificent light and color say good night.

I watch the light slowly fade away.